SHAKTI

The Mystery & Power Of The Divine Life Force

The Magical Tool That Will Leave You Refreshed, Glowing, Enlightened & Above All Make You Feel Very Good In Less Than Sixty Seconds

COPYRIGHT 2009

Sri Vishwanath

www.vish-writer.com

**You can contact the author at
vish@vish-writer.com. You
can also reach him at his US number at
2138142680.**

Dedication

TO LORD KRISHNA, SRI RAMAKRISHNA,
SWAMI VIVEKANANDA & Sharada Devi

First, I want to thank all of you for joining me on this teleseminar. It's a real pleasure to have you at this seminar and I want to congratulate you for being here. We have participants from almost all parts of the world. I just pulled up the list a short while ago. We have people from the USA, Canada, Australia, Malaysia, Singapore, Japan, Hong Kong, UK, Switzerland, Germany, Ireland, Sweden, New Zealand, Saudi Arabia and Dubai. If I missed a few countries, my apologies. I welcome you all to the seminar.

Today's seminar is going to be very special. It's going to completely revamp the way you go about your life from this moment on. I can assure you that you would not be sleeping for the next one week after taking in all that we are going to touch upon today.

We're going to have a live demonstration of getting in touch with the life force(Shakti) which exists within each of us. But before we do that I want to give you a little bit of my background and how I came in contact with this truly remarkable life force.

I've always believed that while knowledge is very good, it doesn't do much good unless it starts making sense in everyday life. It's important that you realize that the revelations I experienced can also come to you.

I'm a human being just like you and if I could get in touch with this life force, so can you. The workings and wonders of spirituality aren't only for monks, priests and other religious persons. These innate endowments can work even better for a normal human being because he/she would be able to immediately see results in their day to day life.

This life force which we're going to talk about today is not privy to a few select individuals who have spent a lot of time in the Himalayan caves or religious schools for one faith or another. This isn't the case. You must understand that this force can be tapped by any individual.

There are some challenges and rules. but they're not obstacles. They don't require you to spend hours in meditation, hold your body in a certain position in a certain place of worship, or worry about impure thoughts. No! All that isn't required at all. Today we're here to fully embrace this life force and explore its tremendous power to transform lives.

Today's seminar is going to be long but there are certain important things to cover. What you'll learn today will last you a lifetime.
So BE ALERT to totally digest the essence and meaning of the life force in you.

So what is this life force?

Let's start with me. I come from a normal middle class family. I'm thirty five years old. I was born and brought up in Mumbai and had a great childhood. I graduated from college with a first class commerce degree and then two earned professional qualifications in finance which is equivalent to the CPA in the United States.

There were very few things my dad refused to buy me, including expensive books I needed at school. He believed a lot in investing in education and so do I. And by taking this teleseminar you show the same faith in education.

Someone is watching what you do, and crediting you for your curiosity and willingness to advance your knowledge. That person is you, and you'll come to realize how significant your investment is.

So coming back to my story, armed

with two professional qualifications, I worked with Fortune 500 companies in India for a couple of years and then landed a plum position in the U.S. In May 1998 at the age of 26 I arrived in the U.S. It was the first time I flew. In December 1998 I married Chitra a devout Indian girl.

Enter The Dragon

In April 1999, shortly after my 27th birthday, something very horrible suddenly happened. I was put in a Pittsburgh hospital for hyper stress, literally fighting for my life. I couldn't eat a morsel of food. It took two hours to finish drinking a glass of water. No doctor could diagnose what had suddenly happened to me. My parents told me to come back to Mumbai and so I and my wife did.

Now understand that until the age of twenty six I hadn't read a single book on self help or spirituality or attended a single lecture on such subjects. But perhaps Nature had something else in store for me.....

It reminds me of Henry Theroux the guy who wrote Walden quote:

"I went to the woods because I wished to live deliberately, to front only the essential facts of life, and see if I could learn what it had to teach, and not, when I came to die, discover that I have not lived.

I spent around twelve months in Mumbai seeing various doctors, psychiatrists, and other specialists. Life was hell for me and for people around me. After three months I resumed work in Mumbai but the stress was enormous. It was affecting every area of my life, which led me to develop a keen interest in spirituality or whatever I understood it to be at that point of time.

Enter The Prince

On June 24th 2000 a light entered into my life. My son Vignesh was born.

I was at the hospital myself at that time. I had one look at my baby son and then went back hurriedly to my room where my mother, my brother, and my brother's wife were. I don't know what happened to me then. But this was my first brush with the life force if I can put it that way. I can clearly remember. I closed my eyes and the moment I did that I started crying loudly like a small child. I had never cried that way. It wasn't a cry of despair but I sensed something was happening inside of me. I could clearly see a blinding flash of light entering into my body and painlessly removing parts of me that I didn't need, that were hurting me, that stopped me from realizing my own strength.

This epiphany went on for minutes before my crying ceased. A powerful life force had surfaced into my mind, one that I hadn't recognized before or had, in my ignorance, ignored before. I couldn't completely understand much of this remarkable experience when it happened to me seven years ago -- but now it makes perfect sense.

Another important thing happened during that week. Since I had taken time off from my work I enrolled for an American public speaking course in Mumbai. It was an intense four day course. It began very well. The speaker was fantastic, and the participants were friendly. My doctor had advised me to carry an emergency pill with me all the time in case I developed stress attacks. For more then eleven months I had tucked it in my front pocket in case I developed stress attacks. I was the first person to make my way out of the door for the tea break and   Guess what !...

Guess what !

I took the packet of pills and threw them in the dustbin, and I've never had need of them since.

It reminds me of a wonderful quote from Dr. Alfred Dsouza which goes something like this:

For a long time it had seemed to me that life was about to begin - real life. But there was always some obstacle in the way. Something to be got through first, some unfinished business, time still to be served, a debt to be paid. Then life would begin, I thought. At last it dawned on me that these obstacles were my life.

I had no clue where I got this strength from when I had been totally down and out. Years later now when I look back at what happened I can say with certainty that it wasn't the speaker or the programme. It was something else which gave me the power.

My health continued to improve and I was on the road to recovery. There was one other important event I forgot to mention to you which happened four days before my son was born. I started chanting a mantra which is a sacred verse in India called the Gayatri Mantra. I used to do this for four hours in the morning. Now remember I had never done this before and four days before his birth I got up at 4.00 am as if someone instructed me to and I sat down and was chanting this mantra for 1008 times for four hours at a stretch. Chanting this mantra, as a recognition of my new-found life force, instilled a sense of strength and power. I could feel its cleansing effect clearly.

Now you don't have to worry about this mantra or anything of this sort. Just imagine that you've never done anything like this before and suddenly you get up and sit at a place and chant for four hours at a stretch. And you do it not for one day but for one whole year four hours daily. All this happened effortlessly and I enjoyed the process. Surely some force might have helped me do that.

I returned to the U.S., went about my work, and life continued as normal. During the next five years I visited various countries as part of my finance consulting profession. During this time I penned around 500 poems and I aspired to become a full time writer on spirituality.

Fast forward to January 12th 2005. A great man entered my life ... John Harricharan. I took a writing course from him and we got along well. From the time I met him my thoughts took a completely different direction. He gave me insightful tips about life and very valuable suggestions in writing for which I'm indebted to him.

Harricharan helped me get in touch with Yanik Silver, a famed Internet marketer. I attended his conference and subsequently created some great products online in the software industry. Within a few months my software website was the number one in the world and there was a good amount of revenue coming in. The funny thing is I couldn't truly comprehend how my site became so successful. Writing books on spirituality was still my main interest. But because this software site did so well I ended up working twelve to fourteen hours a day on it.

I built this website with the hope that it would take care of my expenses so I could concentrate on writing books. giving lectures, and making my presence felt in the spiritual field. But the site was even more successful than I ever hoped. Instead of just taking care of my expenses I was rewarded handsomely. People were buying like crazy and I had no clue what was happening.

ENTER TROUBLE

I owned this website but I had a friend who wrote part of the content. I shared fifty per cent of the revenue with him. But this agreement was based on trust and not a contract. He had no clue of the earnings. In fact, I ended up paying him more than fifty per cent to him out of fear God would punish me if I underpaid him. So my friend, who had been broke, made tons of money as the website did very well. Now the agreement with him was that he would keep writing content on a regular basis so that the website would have updated material. He did that for a few months but from October 2005 he stopped. I continued to send him big cheques every month but he stopped contributing. This situation continued for some time .You know how it is when someone close to you doesn't do things which he/she is supposed to do. People close to you can take you for granted, and often there's little if anything you can do about it.

One day I called my friend to my house and told him this situation couldn't go on. He agreed to resume writing content. For a few days he honored his word but then he went back to not doing anything. It was becoming too frustrating for me.

I had to resolve this bad situation quickly. I sent various communications to him with no response. Then I learned that he was on a holiday with his wife in Sydney. I couldn't take that. Here I was spending 14 hours a day bringing in revenue and this guy wasn't doing a single thing for five months. I sent him a nasty email ending our business relationship. And then began a nightmarish experience for me........ The month of March 2006 was the most horrible month for me.

He wrote back to me saying he was going to sue me. Even though I had a strong case I suddenly felt powerless - - and I don't know why. I felt sad for having fallen into this problem of money. I wanted to get out of it. I was ready to pay whatever was needed to extricate myself from this problem. But my erstwhile friend gave me a hard time. He refused to accept the final share. Here was a guy who I had enriched and I couldn't do anything because for whatever reason I felt powerless as if a pin had pricked the balloon and all the air within me had vanished.

If my parents had known they would have told me to give away the website and the money to him and get away from the scene. This is how I was brought up.

I felt so stupid writing that last email to him. Now remember he had no clue of the earnings. If I was a good bookkeeper I could very easily have gotten out of the situation without making a mess of it. But that wasn't the case and so I suffered.

ENTER THE KING

At this point I would like to introduce to you (as I say this tears roll out from my eyes,) the teachings of Swami Vivekananda, one of the world's greatest philosophers, a person who spent his entire life helping people get in touch with this life force. I have a strong feeling that though he is no longer alive the flash of light which appeared before me five years ago at the time of my son Vignesh's birth resembled his innate presence.

I have a place in my house where I spend around twenty minutes in peace with myself. This is where I connect to the life force or whatever you choose to call this inner voice. My eyes were closed and my hands were folded. Suddenly a thought came to me, ... a six letter word xxxxxx which reminded me that I had inadvertently learned my former friend's email password. I went to the computer, logged in, entered this password, and boom - his email account opened. And what did I see! I saw that he had started a similar website. I couldn't believe it. I had spent a huge amount learning all the Internet marketing skills and during the last year I had revealed everything to him for free, stuffed his pocket with a huge amount of cash. But here he was undercutting me by selling the same product for fifty percent of my price.

Now another terrible part of this situation arose. Another close friend of mine was aware of this problem and had actually joined hands with the other person. The script looked like a Hollywood or Bollywood movie. I knew there are many dirty minds around this world but I had never experienced them. And here I was completely stunned, not knowing what to do. Still, in my naivete, I was discussing this problem to a guy who had already betrayed me.

Since I now had possession of friend's email account, I could have made his life miserable, too. No sooner was I about to take my first step in this direction a powerful thought came:

Stop, Vish! Don't touch him!

I stood there for few minutes not knowing what to do. Then I shut the computer and sat down quietly. Soon I got another thought which told me that the reason I remembered his password *was to help me get out of the problem and not to make his life miserable.* It told me that I should call this other friend of mine who had joined hands with my former partner and use him to get out of the problem. And so I did exactly that.

I called this other friend of mine who didn't know I had discovered his betrayal. We settled at a sum by which I could get out of this whole thing. On March 24th 2006 the matter was finally solved.

Now remember that with all knowledge I had of his unethical dealings I could have crushed my friend and certainly won any court case. But whenever the impulse for vengeance came the same inner voice again would advise:

Stop, Vish! Don't touch him!

This happened about six or seven times. But this voice was so powerful that I didn't have the strength to go ahead. And I thank myself for hearing and listening to that voice.

Over the next few days this voice or this thought also told me: *Don't bother about this site, Vish. I will take care of it. You continue with your work.*

From that day on I've never logged on to my friend's email account even once. I've never visited his site even once. I deleted all the details I had of his unethical activities. *And the best part is I've never spent more than five minutes on my own site from that day on. R*emember I was spending twelve hours on my website until that time. And do you want to know the result......

My revenue doubled for the last year without my spending so much time on the site. Remember I was spending 12 hours earlier. Having listened to this life force voice I was rewarded very handsomely, both financially. and more importantly, with peace of mind. From that point on I've had constant access to this life force. I'm honored to have been blessed by this universe and I'm excited today to have this opportunity to share my experience with you and show how your life force can accomplish similar wonders for you.

It's at this moment right now that the power of the life force will begin in your life. You don't have to wait for a major problem to embrace this life force. The reason I told you about my two crucial life events, one about health and the other about money, was because the best time often to realize your life force is when adversity strikes. *The supreme obstacle is the supreme door.*

Today we will have a live demonstration of this force. At the end of the call you would have got the rare privilege of getting in touch with this force and the process of embracing this life force would have begun.

So are you ready?

I hope everyone has a notepad with them or a sheet of paper that you can write on. You will also need a red and a blue pen. If you do not have colored pens it does not matter just grab hold of a pen or pencil.

Okay, we're are going to have fun now. What I want you to do is to draw a straight line in the middle of the page and divide the page into two so that you now have a right hand side and a left hand side.

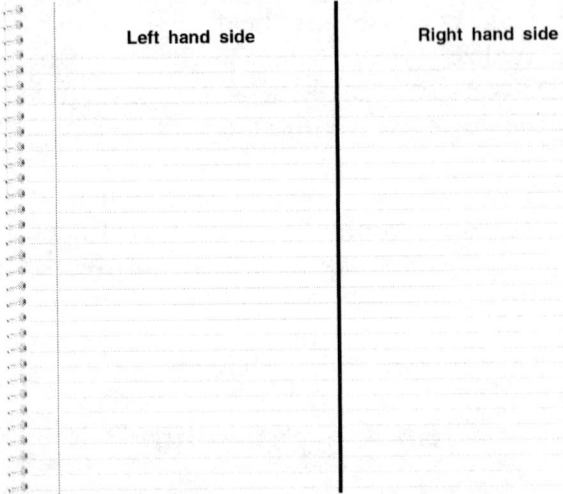

Left hand side	**Right hand side**

Write Experiment Number 1 on the right hand side of the page. Then draw a small arrow below Experiment

No 1 pointing downwards and write *I want to be loved."* Then draw another small arrow below that and write *Physical Experiences*, then draw one last arrow below that and write down *Fantastic Mental Experiences* or you could even write *Feeling Damn Good.*

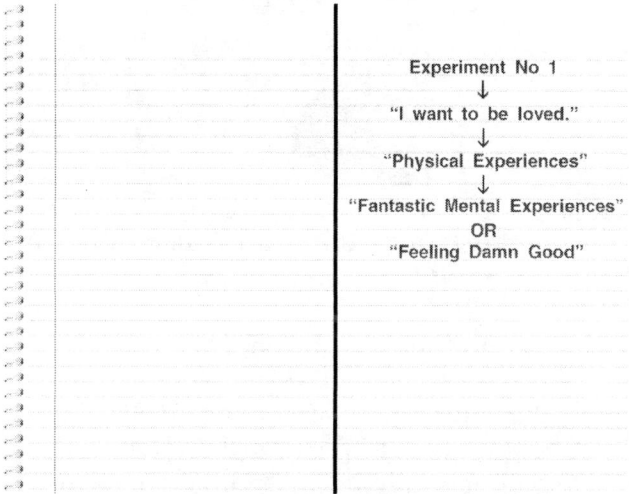

Experiment No 1
↓
"I want to be loved."
↓
"Physical Experiences"
↓
"Fantastic Mental Experiences"
OR
"Feeling Damn Good"

Now for all those who have someone whom you dearly love with you right now, get up and embrace or give a hug to your dear one. Could you do that for me, please.

Take your time and cherish this moment....

So how are you feeling?

I'm sure each of you are feeling good right and if your love for your dear one is really intense you'll soon notice that *you can carry this great feeling* all through the day or perhaps even for some weeks.

Now notice what happened here. You had a wish or desire to be loved which you wrote down on the right hand side and then you had this great physical experience of embrace or hug and that led to a pleasant mental experience of feeling good. Your wish or desire was fulfilled and if the experience was really intense you could sustain that feeling for a long time to come. So far, so good.

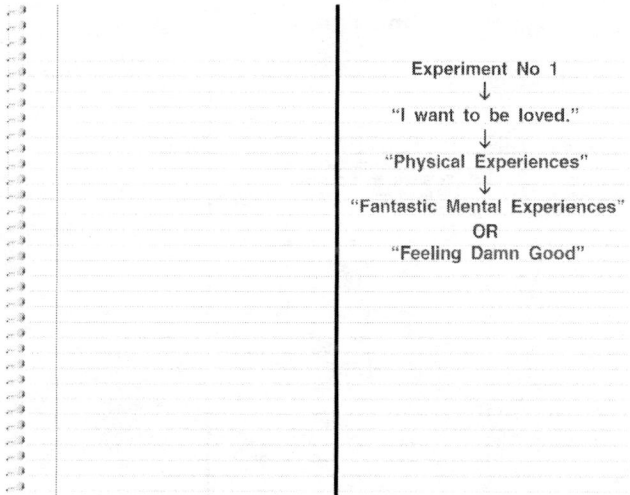

Experiment No 1
↓
"I want to be loved."
↓
"Physical Experiences"
↓
"Fantastic Mental Experiences"
OR
"Feeling Damn Good"

Now comes an even more interesting part.

Write Experiment Number Two on the left hand side of the page. Then draw a small arrow below Experiment No 2 pointing downwards and write "*I want to hold on to an idea about love*" Then draw another small arrow below that and write *I will care About a Wonderful Thought*, then draw one last arrow below that and write down *Fantastic Mental Experiences* or you could even write *Feeling Damn Good.*

Experiment No 2
↓
"I want to hold on an Idea about Love."
↓
"I will care About a Wonderful Thought"
↓
Fantastic Mental Experiences
OR
Feeling Damn Good

So what we're going to do in Experiment No 2 is that you're not going to embrace your loved one. Instead, think of a wonderful thought about your loved one. It could be:

a) Some cherished moments you spent with him or her,

b) A wonderful event in his or her life which you can't forget

c) An intense moment during certain critical times of his or her life which makes your eyes moist

d) One of those pranks you played with him or her or

e) Any thought which you can hold on to ....

Notice what I said "Any thought which you can hold on to." I want you to take that precious thought and give it your complete undivided attention. Notice that if you're really going through these motions as I'm saying this you'll be at complete peace with yourself.

From this moment on your loved one whether he or she is close to you or miles apart will also feel good. *This is because when you care about a loving thought, and give it your undivided attention, the thought gains motion and travels.*

The greater the intensity of your thought the more likely it is that he or she wherever they exist in this universe would receive your thought and would feel good.

If you look back in your life chances are there would be moments when you might have suddenly felt very good. If you were alert you could have sensed that someone who cares about you has sent you a loving thought which you've picked up, with the result that you feel good.

If you notice very carefully in experiment No 2 above, you didn't start with a physical experience. You held on to a wonderful thought about the person whom you cared about. You gave this thought your undivided attention. As you were doing this you were already feeling very good about yourself. The more intensely you firmed up this thought, the more likely it is that your loved one also felt good wherever he or she was. That's the power of a mighty thought. Sitting in one corner of your room you can make yourself and any other person whom you genuinely care about feel very good about themselves.

So now I want you to closely examine your notes.

In Experiment No 1 we had a wish or desire to be loved and so you started with a physical experience of embrace and ended up with what- feeling good

Experiment No 1
↓
"I want to be loved."
↓
"Physical Experiences"
↓
"Fantastic Mental Experiences"
OR
"Feeling Damn Good"

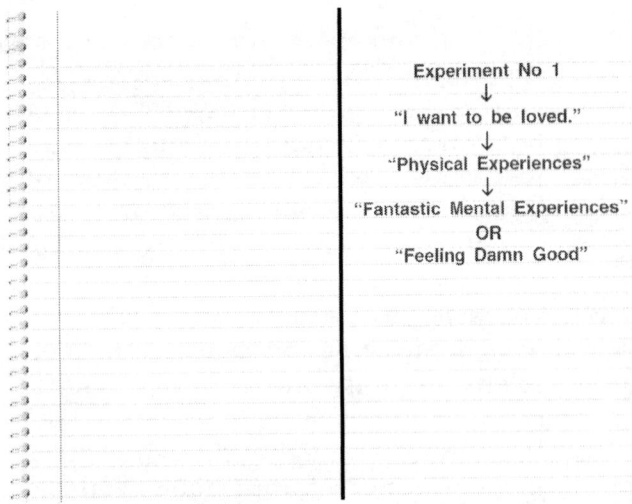

In Experiment No 2 you didn't go through a physical experience. Instead, you started of with a caring thought gave it a lot of undivided attention and also ended up with what ....feeling good.

Experiment No 2
↓
"I want to hold on an
Idea about Love."
↓
"I will care About a
Wonderful Thought"
↓
Fantastic Mental
Experiences
OR
Feeling Damn Good

So have we arrived at the moment of truth, my dear friends?

And the answer is – yes!

What's the highest reward you give to yourself when you have an abundance of wealth, when relationships are at its peak, and when your health is fantastic?

The highest reward about being wealthy, having a great relationship and sound health is feeling content about yourself.

This is the moment of truth. Notice that all our desires and needs culminates in our *feeling good*. That's the highest reward...

It all ends in Feeling very good about yourself.

If you have one million dollars you could buy many things, but the greatest reward it brings is:

You feel very good about yourself.

If you have a great relationship what's the greatest reward it brings with it:

You feel very good about yourself.

If you have the best health in the world, what's the greatest reward it brings with it:

You feel very good about yourself.

So what does all this mean?

Big Secret No 1

It means that problem is not really the lack of money the problem is not really lack of health, the problem is not really lack of relationship the problem is

"I am not feeling really good"

That's the real problem because all these things ultimately lead you to that one thing: about feeling very good.

If you're having problems with relationships you might feel that if you could find or attract a wonderful partner into your life who can understand you your whole life would change and you would start feeling good about yourself.

If you have problems with money you might feel that once you have a million dollars in your bank account you could buy many things and feel good about yourself.

If you have problems with health you might feel that once you're able to get over your illness you would be cheerful and happy....

If you refine a problem what do you notice immediately?

That the only problem is about not feeling currently good. The good news about all this is that feeling good is a fantastic mental experience which doesn't require you to hold on to anything physical.

Look what's happening here. You feel that you need a physical experience to go from the point of feeling low to the point of feeling good But this isn't totally true because in experiment no 2 you arrived at the same result without going through the physical experience, and you still felt very good.

Here's the blinding moment of truth:

Big Secret No 2

Whenever you're at the right hand side of the page you'll feel that you're missing something in life. You'll always be after something because you'll feel that life is incomplete.

But every time that you're on the left hand side, how did you feel? For those moments there was nothing missing in your life.

So understand this: Instead of starting from a point of feeling incomplete and low about yourself, begin from the point of feeling complete about yourself like the way you did in experiment number two. Say to yourself:

Yes, there is a need about money, a

need to improve my health, and to develop better relationships. I'll take care of all this but I'm still alive and have come here so far.

Many times the universe works in the background for us so we don't see everything that affects us. But the fact is we've been alive for so many years and are already complete.

There's nothing wrong in you because one wonderful moment can make you feel good just the way we did in experiment number two. You are just one moment away from getting out of your lack of money, health or relationship problem. And I will show you how.

The Magic Begins

When you start from the point of being complete with yourself a strange decision making power surrounds you. You're sure that the universe or this higher force will take care of you and that you're just a moment away from having your problems solved. So always be on the left hand side, my dear friends.

You're not really missing anything in life. You're fine at this point. Did you hear what I said "You are perfectly fine right now as you are." You are complete. Any person in the world can start feeling real good by understanding that he or she is complete; and then by holding on to an idea about money, health or relationships with undivided attention you can make that eventually lead to a successful outcome. That's the greatest secret.

So the next biggest question is how do we feel good when everything around us is going in exactly the opposite way?

And that brings up another interesting question:

How can nature be so serene and majestic when there are so many horrible events like earthquakes, tornadoes, and other disasters?

And the answer is that it isn't nature which is peaceful but the energy which envelops mountains and the oceans and makes it seem tranquil. It's this same energy which exists in every being in this universe, be it in nature or with human beings. It's only the degree of manifestation which differs. Nature is aware that it's complete in itself but we're not. *We just have to acknowledge the fact that we are complete.*

So what is this energy we're talking

about which runs the whole universe?

This energy is what is called "The Life Force or Shakti." Once you have got in touch with this life force your life will never be the same again.

What I want you to do now is write on the right hand side of the page-
"I am the Body "; below that write that "I am the Mind"; and below it write "I am the thoughts."

I am the Body
↓
I am the Mind
↓
I am the thoughts

Now on the left hand side of the page write "I am the Energy" and "I am the Life Force."

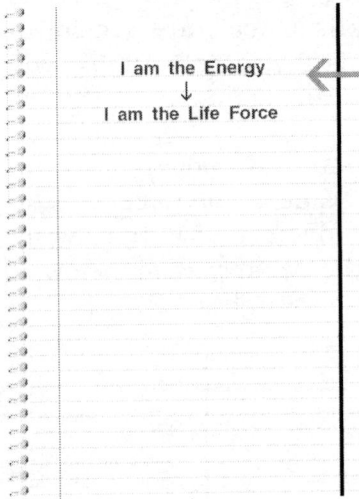

I am the Energy
↓
I am the Life Force

Now go back to Experiment No 2 where you took the warm thoughts about the person whom you loved. At that heightened moment you had completely forgotten about yourself. You had entered into a field which was complete by itself and you felt good. Weren't you completely at peace with yourself when you merged with that loving thought? Didn't you feel a new and comforting feeling?

Whenever you feel damn good, and I'm not talking about the ordinary moments but extraordinary ones, you'll notice that something *fills you up* and this something is not your body or your mind or your thoughts.

This space that you enter into has got only one thing and that is energy, vibrant energy circulating within which we call "The life force." If you're alert you'll notice that during those intense moments you weren't aware about your body or mind. Your energy came in direct contact with the energy of the universe, creating a blissful moment to watch out for. Your body and mind become merged with the energy of the universe. *It made you feel good because it is in the nature of this energy, this life force, to feel good.*

You'll notice that the moment you come out of this extraordinary experience the next thought is waiting there for you. Notice what I said "the next thought is waiting there for you" and the moment you pick this next thought up you're back to your regular thought patterns.

Right at this moment if you eliminate your body and mind, what do you think exists in that space surrounding you? Nothing but energy, the life force. Before you came it existed and after you leave it will exist. If you disintegrate your body and mind, all that remains is energy.

Your real nature is that of energy, and this life force is complete by itself. It's capable of giving you exactly those things which you require but you need to get your body and mind primed to realize this life force in you.

The next big question that pops up is "How do we as human beings become aware of this fact that we are the energy and the life force?." And this is the last piece of puzzle in this whole game.

Big Secret No 3

Notice that every time that you're on the right hand side of the page you become aware of the fact that "You are the Body, You are Mind, and You are the Thought" and you feel that something is missing. Many times you might feel low.

I am the Body
↓
I am the Mind
↓
I am the thoughts

Whenever you're on the left hand side of the page you automatically become aware of the fact that "You are the Energy, You are the life force, You are complete" -- and a strange feeling of goodness comes to you .

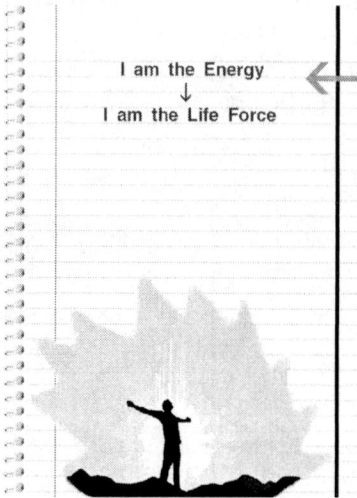

I am the Energy
↓
I am the Life Force

How do you strengthen the thought that you are the energy and the life force?

This is how you do it. Write down "Release Points" on the right hand side of the page and circle it.

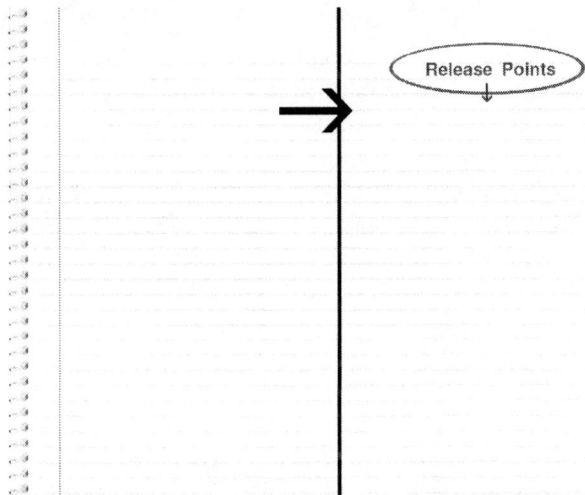

If you are the energy and life force, what is the first thing you need to do?

You must watch how you're using your energy from the moment you get up in the morning. You bang your energy into bodies, you enter into bodies, exit out of bodies you get in touch with people get in touch with their minds look where you are applying your energy all day.

When you are alone you bang it with your same old thoughts. All day you utilize your energy in former ways and never really come to know your true nature. You remain on the right hand side of the page and your life becomes a drag.

Now write down "Where do I Bang My Energy" below Release Points on the right hand side of the page.

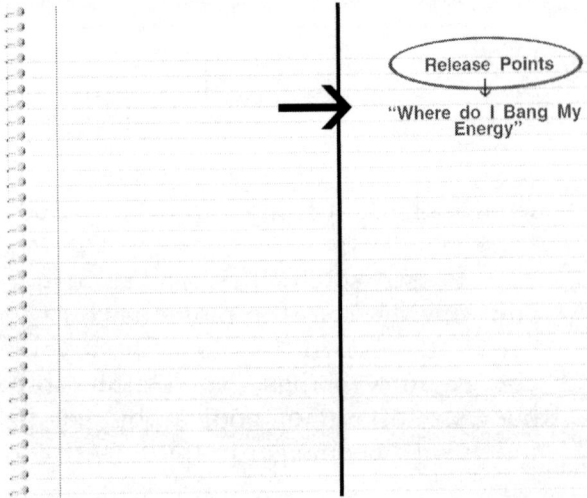

Release Points

"Where do I Bang My Energy"

Let's do a small hands on exercise here.

Write down all those things you do when you feel low, when you are engulfed with problems.
Do you go for a drink?

Do you smoke?

Phone friends?

Do you have or look for sex?

Do you go to the movies?

Switch on television?

Do you go to pubs?

Again I'm not saying these things are good or bad. All I'm saying is you must be aware how you're treating the life force. And you can notice something interesting here. Whenever you utilize your energy, the feel the good factor which comes out of it doesn't last long. Whatever you do to alleviate your low periods, the feel good factor evaporates when that time period ends and you can't hold on to it.

But that isn't the case when you're on the left hand side of the page because you saw that just one embrace of your loved one for sixty seconds could last for much longer periods. All you had to do was to hold on to it and you would feel very good.

What I want you to do now is to write on the left hand side of the page a few of the activities which will help you become aware of this life force and draw you closer to it. These are just a few suggestions and you can add to this list.

- Spend time with nature. Any activity which allows you to get in touch with nature is the best deal.

- Go for a long walk. The intention of this walk is to take

- your life force for a walk like you take your dog for a walk. This has benefited me tremendously. Whenever I feel very low I go for a long walk. I go alone. I acknowledge the problem and instead of ignoring or misusing my energy I relish having this great gift-- this life Force. The moment I become aware of it I know that "I am complete." I realize that what problem troubles me is something which will pass away in due time but the life force will remain.

- Read books that elevate the mind and spirit. Hold on to something in the book which will help you to remember that you are the life force. It could be a small quote, a sentence, or anything in the book. If any of you are interested in the books I read you can send me an email at vish@vish-writer.com

- Take up any sport. I always believe that instead of watching sports you got to play it. Being from Mumbai I used to watch cricket 10 hours a day until I stopped doing that 2 yrs back .Go for a swim, play tennis, play base ball, play basketball, play ice hockey, play whatever game you want sport is excellent but play the sport watch the sport less very less and you will see that as you play more and watch less you make your life interesting.

- Watch select movies. The problem is when your emotional level becomes too heightened which will put you on the right hand side. The emotional level of consciousness only has human intelligence embedded into it. It can't get in touch with the life force. It will always make you feel that there is something missing and that you have to get it, whatever that it is.

We're all emotional by nature which is fine but we have this great privilege that we are also honored by this miraculous intelligence of the universe. You can get in touch with this life force when you heighten your deep feelings, and not your emotions.

This is a long discussion but just to cut it short there's a huge difference between emotions and deep feelings. Your job is to heighten your deep feelings and not your emotions. I watch movies like Lion King, Nemo, Brother Bear, Blizzard, Happy Feet, The Chronicles of Narnia and in all these movies my deep feelings are heightened.

Whenever I watch a typical Hollywood movie I would most likely miss the message and get too involved in the personalities in the film. The end result would be that it would only stir up my emotions. So you need to be choosy about the movies you watch.

Go for movies which heighten your deep feelings and which help you to remember to be on the left hand side of the page. Play with your feelings. Watch your feelings mature, and see how they become a force on their own.

Friends, whenever you're on the left hand side you make your life interesting. *Whenever you're on the right hand side. you're probably making other people's lives interesting.* Just remember: you're complete by yourself. Don't be fooled into rushing towards everything. Watch your release points.

When you misuse or neglect your life force, you can expand the sensation of a void in your life that you'll feel by not properly employing your energy.

When you do the things we talked about right now you hold on to a tool which is real and not illusionary. It's vital that you remember that you are actually the life force. The moment you do so a strange feeling of goodness comes to you and you know it's real. All you have to do is be on the left hand side of the page and you're safe.

One last thing and very important thing. You don't have to be on the left hand side of the page for the whole day, not even for 12 hours not even for 2 hours not even for an hour not even for thirty minutes.. Recall Experiment No 2 . All you did was have a loving thought for sixty seconds and look at the result. You felt so good. That is all you need to do. *It's the intensity of the thought and not how long the thought lasts* which will produce this great feeling of merging with the life force.

Remember each day to be on the left hand side of the page, and that you are the life force, and the rest will follow.

Take a step back when considering problems and you can automatically fall into the left hand side. Hold on to this thought of withdrawal and your life force will soon triumph.

The question is: How many times can you withdraw? The more times you do this, the more you fall into the left hand side. The more activities you do in tandem with your life force, you become aware of being aligned with your energy and how complete you are.

I am the Energy
↓
I am the Life Force

The more you withdraw the more such behavior becomes a good habit that enriches your life, spares you aggravation, and puts you in touch with your life force. The more you get to the left hand side of the page the more it will become a habit and very soon it will become natural and will come easy to you. It will become a part of you, or rather you become the life force

So remember always:

1. That the problem is not about lack of money, lack of love, or lack of sound health; the problem is about feeling good.

2. You feel good when you are complete.

3. Understand that you are the life force and that the nature of the life force is one of being complete. Therefore, there is nothing missing in your life.

4 The life force knows exactly what you want and it will help you in achieving those goals. All you have to do is acknowledge that you are the life force and allow the vibrant energy of this force to take over your life.

5. How do you acknowledge this life force? *By watching your "Release points" and withdrawing to the left hand side of the page as many times as you can during the day.* Do this by picking up an activity such as spending time with nature, going for a long walk, reading selective books, watching selective movies, playing sports, ecetera. Make that a habit which will help you remember to be on the left hand side of the page.

6. Every time that you get on to the left hand side of the page hold on the thought which led you there. So if you can't hold on to money, hold on to an idea about money; if you can't hold on to love, hold on to an idea about love; and if you can't hold on to sound health, hold on to an idea about sound health.

7. Only after you have finished steps one through six, and you have hopped on to the left hand side of the page and you feel real good, should you then think about your current issues and problems.

8. It takes only a few seconds to go from the point of feeling low to the point of feeling good. It takes little time to finish step one through six.

All you need is an intense thought as in Experiment Number Two.

A thought gains strength when you think about it again and again. When you follow these simple rules a *strange decision making* circle will eventually form around you, which will guide you both during good and bad times. It's a wonderful and fantastic changeover that will electrify your life. Go for it, my dear friends. Go for it!

When you play with this life force, life plays with you.

When you respect this life force the universe opens its magical door for you.

The heavens are great and wonderful but far greater and wonderful are the heavens within. It's these Edens that await you. God bless and thank you.